HINDU
FESTIVALS AND TRADITIONS

by Anita Ganeri

PEBBLE
a capstone imprint

Published by Pebble, an imprint of Capstone
1710 Roe Crest Drive, North Mankato, Minnesota 56003
capstonepub.com

Copyright © 2025 by Capstone. All rights reserved. No part of this publication may be reproduced in whole or in part, or stored in a retrieval system, or transmitted in any form or by any means, electronic, mechanical, photocopying, recording, or otherwise, without written permission of the publisher.

Library of Congress Cataloging-in-Publication Data is available on the Library of Congress website.
ISBN: 9780756594497 (hardcover)
ISBN: 9780756594541 (paperback)
ISBN: 9780756594534 (ebook PDF)

Summary: Hindu people live all over the world, and they celebrate festivals and special days in many ways. Discover the traditions, celebrations, and histories behind Diwali, Holi, Raksha Bandhan, and other important Hindu days.

Editorial Credits
Designer: Dina Her; Media Researcher: Jo Miller; Production Specialist: Tori Abraham

Image Credits
Alamy: Dinodia Photos, 15, Cbuchananstock, 27, CPA Media Pte Ltd, 21; Getty Images: Manoj Bainda, 6, Mayur Kakade, 28, partha dalal photography, 18, triloks, 5; Newscom: JANE TYSKA/MCT, 25; Shutterstock: Attitude, background (throughout), Creative Minds2, 14, Dipak Shelare, cover (top), Kristin F. Ruhs, 9, Mahendra Waghamare, 10, StockImageFactory.com, 1, 22, THIANTHAI, 13, Toa55, cover (bottom), 17

Any additional websites and resources referenced in this book are not maintained, authorized, or sponsored by Capstone. All product and company names are trademarks™ or registered® trademarks of their respective holders.

Printed and bound in China. 6098

TABLE OF CONTENTS

Introduction to Hinduism......................4

Holi 7

Raksha Bandhan 12

Diwali 16

Life Events 24

    Glossary 30

    Read More 31

    Internet Sites............................. 31

    Index 32

    About the Author 32

Words in **bold** are in the glossary.

INTRODUCTION TO HINDUISM

At least 4,000 years ago, a religion called Hinduism began in India. Most Hindus believe a great spirit called Brahman is the force behind the whole universe. They worship many **deities**. Each represents different powers and qualities of Brahman.

Today, Hinduism is the third-largest religion in the world. Most Hindus live in India, but many have settled around the world. The Hindu year is filled with festivals and celebrations. Many are tied to Hindu **mythology**.

Hinduism is the oldest established religion in the world.

The Holi bonfire represents good triumphing over evil.

Holi

February or March welcomes the first night of Holi, the Hindu festival of colors. People gather around huge bonfires. The light from the fire marks the end of winter and the beginning of spring. It also shows how good shines through the darkness of evil.

In Hindu mythology, the holiday is tied to the story of a wicked woman. The god Vishnu helps a young prince defeat her.

The next day, the real fun begins. In the morning, people rush into the streets. They shower each other in colorful powders mixed with water.

Soon, everyone is covered in bright pinks, greens, yellows, and blues. A person's social rank or background does not matter. Everyone gets splashed!

Throwing colors at each other reminds Hindus of a story about the mischievous god Krishna. He loved playing tricks on his friends!

The powder used at Holi is a mixture of cornstarch and dye.

9

Coconut barfi is a soft kind of sweet. Some people say it tastes like fudge.

Holi celebrations get very messy! By the end of the day, everyone is soaking wet. They change into dry, clean clothes. Then they go out to visit family and friends. Everyone says, "Happy Holi!"

Guests bring gifts of Indian sweets. A popular sweet is coconut **barfi**. It is made from milk, sugar, and chopped coconut. It is very, very sweet! People make the treats at home or buy them from sweet shops.

RAKSHA BANDHAN

The festival of Raksha Bandhan falls at the end of August. This is when brothers and sisters show their love for each other. In a Hindu family, cousins count as siblings too!

In **Sanskrit**, *Raksha* means "protection." *Bandhan* means "to tie." Hindus tell a story about Indra, king of the gods. Before Indra fought evil demons, his wife tied a silk bracelet around his wrist to keep him safe.

Indra is the god of war. It is also believed he controls the weather.

During Raksha Bandhan, a sister ties a special bracelet around her brother's right wrist to protect him from harm. In return, the brother gives his sister a gift and promises to look after her. Chocolates, jewelry, and money are common gifts.

Rakhis come in a variety of colors, and customers can choose their favorites.

The bracelet is called a rakhi. Traditionally, rakhis were simple pieces of cotton thread. Today, there are many colorful designs decorated with ribbons, tinsel, and sequins.

15

DIWALI

In October or November, Hindus celebrate the festival of Diwali. It is one of the happiest times in the Hindu year. Wherever Hindus have settled in the world, they join in the Diwali fun.

In India, Diwali lasts for five days. In other countries, it may be held over a weekend. On the first day, people clean their homes and decorate them with bright **rangoli** patterns. They go shopping for food and new clothes.

Rangoli designs use sand, rocks, flower petals, rice flour, and other brightly colored dry materials.

Diyas traditionally use nut or seed oil as fuel.

Diwali is also known as the festival of lights. Inside and out, Hindus light up their homes and **mandirs** with rows of **diyas**. The diyas show that light is more powerful than darkness, and that good always wins over evil.

The diyas also welcome the goddess Lakshmi into people's homes. She is the goddess of wealth and good fortune. People pray for her to bless their families and friends.

During Diwali, people retell the story of the god Rama. Long ago, Rama and his wife, Sita, had to leave their homeland. For many years, they lived in the forest.

One day, an evil demon kidnapped Sita and carried her away. Rama killed the demon and rescued Sita. After that, the couple was able to go home. People lit diyas to guide them safely back. In Indonesia, the tale is told using shadow puppets. In the United States, skits or dances tell the story.

Rama's battle with the demon is one of the best-known Hindu stories.

Fireworks, diyas, lanterns, and sparklers all add to the festival of lights.

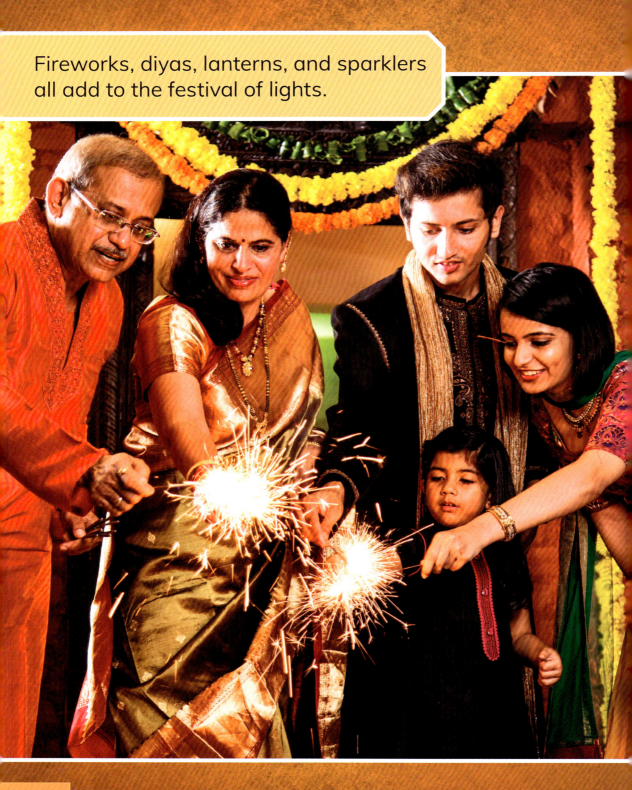

22

Having fun with friends and family is all part of Diwali. People dress up and go to parties. They exchange cards and gifts. They eat sweets, such as almond barfi. The special sweet is shaped into a diamond and coated with silver leaf. The night ends with spectacular fireworks displays.

Although Diwali is a Hindu festival, it is also an important celebration for Sikhs. In India, Jains and Buddhists join in the fun too. More than a billion people around the world celebrate the festival of lights.

LIFE EVENTS

No matter where they live, Hindus have special traditions to mark key times in their lives. When a Hindu baby is 40 days old, he or she is usually taken to the mandir for a naming ceremony. The priest announces the baby's name and says prayers for a long life.

Some Hindu babies are named after gods and goddesses, characters from myths, or holy places. Some are named after important qualities. For example, the name Priya means "lovable." But some babies are named after famous Indian film stars!

A naming ceremony can also be done at home.

Hindus do not consider death to be the end. Instead, a person's soul lives on in a new body. A person's next life depends on this one. Good deeds mean a better life. Bad behavior means the next life will be worse.

When a Hindu dies, the body is **cremated** on a **pyre**. The eldest son, or a close relative, lights the fire. A **pujari** says prayers. People mourn for at least 10 days. On the last day, they believe the soul goes to its next life.

In Bali, the deceased person rests inside a wooden animal, such as a bull, a fish with an elephant's head, or a winged lion.

Each step the newlyweds take represents one of the seven promises they make to each other.

A wedding is a very happy time in the Hindu year. Celebrations can last for several days. A pujari leads the ceremony and lights the sacred fire. The bride and groom do not speak to each other. A white cloth placed between them means they cannot look at each other either.

The most important part of the ceremony is when the couple takes seven steps around the sacred fire. With each step, they make a vow. These vows are for good food, good health, wealth, good fortune, children, happiness, and life-long friendship.

GLOSSARY

barfi (BERR-fee)—a type of Indian sweet made from milk, sugar, and chopped nuts

cremate (KREE-mate)—to burn a dead body to ashes

deity (DEE-uh-tee)—a god or goddess

diya (DEE-ah)—a small lamp made from a clay bowl filled with oil

mandir (mun-DEER)—a Hindu temple

mythology (mi-THOL-uh-jee)—old or ancient stories told again and again that help connect people with their past

pujari (poo-JAR-ee)—a Hindu priest

pyre (PYER)—a pile of wood built to burn a dead body for a funeral

rangoli (rang-GO-lee)—a colorful design drawn with sand, rice, or other materials

Sanskrit (SAN-skrit)—an ancient Indian language

Read More

Andrews, Elizabeth. *Diwali*. Minneapolis: DiscoverRoo, an imprint of Pop!, 2024.

Memtombi, R. K. *Diwali*. Minneapolis: Core Library, an imprint of Abdo Publishing, 2024.

Ramkumar, Ranjeeta. *Holi*. North Mankato, MN: Capstone, 2024.

Internet Sites

Hinduism for Kids
gunatitjyot.org/about/hinduism/hinduism-for-kids

Kiddle: Hinduism Facts for Kids
kids.kiddle.co/Hinduism

National Geographic Kids: India
kids.nationalgeographic.com/geography/countries/article/india

INDEX

babies, 24
bonfires, 6, 7
Brahman, 4

clothes, 11, 16
colored powders, 8, 9

death, 26, 27
Diwali, 16, 19, 20, 23
diyas, 18, 19, 20, 22

fireworks, 22, 23
food, 10, 11, 14, 16, 23, 29

gifts, 11, 14, 23

Holi, 6, 7, 9, 11

Indra, 12, 13

Krishna, 8

Lakshmi, 19

mythology, 4, 7, 24

rakhis, 15
Raksha Bandhan, 12, 14
Rama, 20, 21
rangoli patterns, 16, 17

Sita, 20

Vishnu, 7

weddings, 28, 29

ABOUT THE AUTHOR

Anita Ganeri is an award-winning author of children's books. She was born in Kolkata, India, but now lives in Britain. She writes on many topics, but India is her favorite!